SOME SWELL PUP

SOME SWELL PUP

or Are You Sure You Want a Dog?

Story by *Maurice Sendak* and *Matthew Margolis*
Pictures by *Maurice Sendak*

PictureLions
An Imprint of HarperCollins*Publishers*

First published in the USA by Farrar,
Straus & Giroux, New York in 1976
First published in Great Britain by
The Bodley Head Children's Books 1976
First published in Picture Lions in 1992

Picture Lions is an imprint of the Children's Division,
part of HarperCollins Publishers Limited,
77-85 Fulham Palace Road, Hammersmith,
London W6 8JB

ISBN: 0 00 664087-7

Printed in Hong Kong

For Connie, Erda, Io, and Aggie M.S.
For my son, Jesse M.M.

ONE HOUR LATER . . .

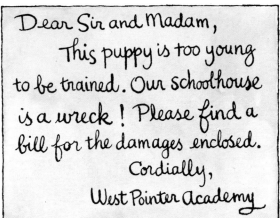

AND SO, NEXT DAY . . .

THAT NIGHT . . .

SO THEY WENT TO SLEEP AND DREAMED . . .

THE GIRL'S DREAM

AND IN THE MORNING . . .

SO...